FEB – 1 2017

CUTTING-EDGE TECHNOLOGY

LASERS

James Bow

Gareth Stevens
PUBLISHING

Please visit our website, **www.garethstevens.com**.
For a free color catalog of all our high-quality books,
call toll free 1-800-542-2595 or fax 1-877-542-2596.

Cataloging-in-Publication Data

Names: Bow, James.
Title: Lasers / James Bow.
Description: New York : Gareth Stevens Publishing, 2017. | Series: Cutting-edge technology | Includes index.
Identifiers: ISBN 9781482451641 (pbk.) | ISBN 9781482451580 (library bound) | ISBN 9781482451467 (6 pack)
Subjects: LCSH: Lasers–Juvenile literature.
Classification: LCC TA1682.B69 2017 | DDC 621.36'6–dc23

First Edition

Published in 2017 by
Gareth Stevens Publishing
111 East 14th Street, Suite 349
New York, NY 10003

Produced for Gareth Stevens by Calcium
Editors: Sarah Eason and Harriet McGregor
Designer: Jessica Moon
Picture researcher: Harriet McGregor

Picture credits: Cover: Shutterstock: kadmy (photo), Shutterstock: Eky Studio (banner), Shutterstock: R-studio (back
cover bkgrd); Insides: Creative Works, Inc. (www.thewoweffect.com) 25; NASA: NASA's Goddard Space Flight Center
Scientific Visualization Studio 37; Shutterstock: Anyaivanova 21, Asharkyu 28, Bildagentur Zoonar GmbH 45, Alexander
Gospodinov 5, Imfoto 13, Sanchai Khudpin 33, Lightpoet 27, Gardar Olafsson 34, Anita Ponne 7, Fouad A. Saad 9;
Wikimedia Commons: 39, Creative Tools from Halmdstad, Sweden 41, Directed Energy Directorate/U.S. Air Force
31, ESO/Yuri Beletsky 42, Damien Jemison/LLNL 1, Krorc 19, LLNL 17t, NASA 17b, 23, Tatoute 11, U.S. Army Space &
Missile Defense Command 14.

Printed in the United States of America
CPSIA compliance information: Batch #CS16GS: For further information contact Gareth Stevens, New York, New York at 1-800-542-2595.

CONTENTS

CHAPTER 1

INCREDIBLE LASERS

Over the last 100 years, technology has changed the world in ways that people could once hardly have imagined. However, all of our inventions, from the 3-D printer to maglev trains, started when somebody was inspired to imagine, investigate, and experiment. From these discoveries, technologies were invented that changed the way people lived. Lasers are one of the incredible cutting-edge technologies that have transformed our world.

WHAT IS A LASER?

Lasers are rays of light energy that people use in many different areas of their lives. The word "laser" means "Light Amplification by Stimulated Emission of Radiation." "Amplification" means that the power of the light has been increased. "Stimulated Emission of Radiation" means that energy has been added to the radiation, making it more powerful. Grocery stores have lasers to read barcodes, the police use lasers to measure distance and speed, and lasers can even join **atoms** together. It is hard to believe that 100 years ago, lasers did not even exist!

In this book, we will look at how lasers work and how scientists invented them. We will show how lasers have changed the way we live and the incredible things lasers have made possible.

LASER BEAMS

Science fiction often shows laser beams shooting around and causing damage. However, it is not usually possible to see laser beams, until they hit something. Light travels in one direction, and it has to hit something, such as a wall or dust, to scatter and be reflected, or bounced, toward your eyes so you can see it. Laser beams can be seen in the same way.

Laser beams are concentrated beams of light. They focus a lot of light on a small space. This can create beautiful light shows or burn holes in things.

The journey to understanding lasers began with the study of light. Early scientists studied light by observing it. They could see light as a beam shining into a darkened room through an opening in a curtain. They could amplify, or make stronger, sunlight by shining it through a magnifying glass, producing a point of light so hot it could burn. They began to understand that light was something they could work with.

SPLITTING LIGHT

In 1666, Sir Isaac Newton (1642–1727) shone a beam of white light through a prism, which is a triangular-shaped wedge of glass. He split the light into the colors of the rainbow. He showed that light moves like waves and that the different colors of light are moving at different **wavelengths**. When light waves hit a prism, the glass changes the direction of the light. The different wavelengths bend in slightly different directions, and so all the colors separate.

LIGHT AS ENERGY

In 1845, Michael Faraday (1791–1867) was working with electricity and **magnetism** when he discovered that these forces could be used to change light. This was called the Faraday Effect. It suggested that light was a form of energy, like **electromagnetism**. Faraday's friend, James Clerk Maxwell (1831–1879), proved this to be true 30 years later. Light is part of a larger spectrum, or range, of energy. The longer the wavelength, the lower the energy. Infrared light, microwaves, and radio waves have longer wavelengths than visible light. Ultraviolet light, x-rays, and gamma rays have shorter wavelengths than visible light. The shorter the wavelength, the higher the energy of the wave.

When a light beam bends when traveling from one substance to another it is called refraction. Here, white light refracts as it moves from air to glass. It splits into the colors of the rainbow.

ENERGY WAVES

Waves of energy are a series of peaks and dips, like waves moving along the surface of water. The space between two of the peaks is called a wavelength. When these peaks are close together, the wavelengths are shorter. They are said to have a higher **frequency**. When the peaks are farther apart, there is less energy, and the wavelengths are longer. They have a lower frequency.

THE POWER OF LIGHT

Although we have talked about wavelengths of light, Newton believed that light was a small piece of matter called a particle. Scientists have argued about the question of whether light is a wave or a particle for centuries.

WAVES OR PARTICLES

Light acts like a wave. It bends, like water does, when a wave hits a narrow opening in a wall. To see this in action, stand in front of a bright light and place your hands together, palms facing toward you, so they are between you and the light. Do you notice the dark lines in the gap between your hands? That is waves of light bending as they come through the gap, producing spots where there is no wave and no light. However, light also acts like a particle. It bounces off surfaces like a rubber ball and moves in straight lines.

PHOTONS

In 1900, German physicist Max Planck (1858–1947) suggested light was both a wave and a particle. He thought that "lumps" of light could gain or lose energy. Planck put together an equation that explained how much energy light could lose depending on its wavelength. The great physicist Albert Einstein (1875–1955) used this equation to explain how light produced electricity. The American physicist Gilbert Lewis (1875–1946) then named these light particles "photons."

Now that scientists knew light was made of photons and that it was related to electricity and magnetism, they could use energy to change light and amplify it. They started to use the power of light as a tool. Study of infrared lasers began in the 1950s. At first, scientists found it very difficult to create laser light.

When light waves have to travel through a small opening, they spread out in circles as they pass out of the opening. This is called diffraction.

THE MASER

The first laser was invented in 1954, but because laser light is so difficult to create, it did not use light at all. Instead it used microwaves and was called a Maser. To create an energy beam, American inventor Charles Townes (1915–2015) and his coworkers used electricity to excite a stream of ammonia **molecules**, producing microwaves. Scientists worked hard to improve the first laser, and on May 16, 1960, American physicist Theodore Maiman (1927–2007) was the first to create a laser that produced visible light.

CHAPTER 2

USING THE LIGHT

Laser light is different from regular light. Regular light is made up of many different wavelengths and colors. It scatters all over the place. This is why when you turn on a light bulb, you see everything in a room. You feel the heat from sunlight, but until you concentrate it using a magnifying glass to create a point of light, you will not catch fire.

A laser pumps a lot of energy to make light. It produces light that is tuned to a narrow wavelength, and it concentrates all of that energy in a tight beam. Laser light does not scatter. With all of that energy concentrated in a small area, a lot of light can be sent into a small space quickly. Once the light hits something, if there is enough energy, it can burn it.

PARTS OF A LASER

A laser is usually made of three parts. A pump source provides energy. This could be electricity, a **chemical reaction**, or even another laser. The **gain medium** creates the laser light. The energy from the pump source travels through the gain medium, which can be a liquid, a gas, or a solid

CUTTING EDGE

Chemical lasers use a chemical reaction to provide the laser's power. Hydrogen-fluoride lasers use streams of hydrogen gas mixed with fluoride. When the hydrogen and fluoride mix, they create an explosion. This makes a huge amount of energy that can be turned into laser light.

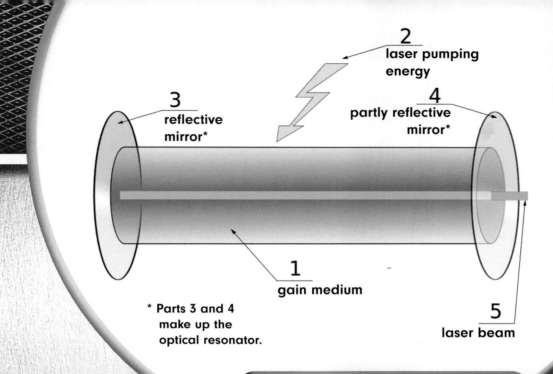

3
reflective
mirror*

4
partly reflective
mirror*

1
gain medium

* Parts 3 and 4
make up the
optical resonator.

5
laser beam

A laser works by pumping energy from a source through a gain medium. The gain medium tunes the energy so that when it leaves the optical resonator, it has a particular wavelength.

crystal. The atoms of the gain medium tune the light energy as it passes through, the same way that light traveling through colored glass takes on the color of the glass, but much more precisely.

Finally, there is an optical resonator. The simplest version of this is two mirrors on either side of the gain medium. One mirror is reflective and lets through a lot of light. The other is partly reflective and only lets through some light. Energy travels from the pump source through the gain medium, where it is tuned to a particular wavelength. The energy bounces back and forth between the two mirrors before escaping through the partly reflective mirror as laser light.

Another type of laser is a gas laser, in which electricity is run through gas to produce laser light. The electricity excites the gas molecules in the gain medium, making them vibrate, or move back and forth rapidly. The laser then uses the vibrations to tune the energy pumped in from the pump source to create a particular wavelength of light.

GAS LASERS

Physicists William Bennett Jr. (1930–2008) and Ali Javan (born 1926) used helium and neon to create the first gas laser in 1960. It produced a concentrated infrared light beam. Carbon dioxide, carbon monoxide, and krypton gas can be used to produce a wide range of laser light. Lasers that use vapors of copper produce some of the most powerful lasers.

SOLID-STATE LASERS

A solid-state laser is a laser that uses a solid gain medium. Light passes through the solid, such as glass or crystal. Other material is added as a "**dopant**." The dopant changes how the glass or crystal affects the energy passed through it.

The first solid-state lasers, produced in 1960, used rubies as their gain medium. The chromium in the ruby crystal tunes the energy of the pump source, creating laser light of a certain wavelength. Solid-state lasers can use other materials. Rare earth elements, such as holmium, thulium, or erbium, can be used to produce higher energy beams of light.

Solid-state lasers are easier to build than gas lasers because gas can sometimes be poisonous. Solid-state lasers produce a narrower beam than most gas lasers. They also make a lot of power from a relatively small amount of energy. However, their gain mediums can become very hot and the lasers lose power.

Aluminum oxide is usually a white mineral. Chromium adds the red color, making it a ruby.

GEMSTONES

Crystals such as rubies are used to make solid-state lasers, but, in general, gemstones cannot make laser light. Solid-state materials like gemstones are usually man-made and are shaped a little like glass tubes. These shapes are not suitable for making a laser beam because they bend and scatter light too much.

LIQUID LASERS

Liquid dyes can also be used as a gain medium. A liquid dye is a **solvent**, which is a mixture of **organic** molecules in water or alcohol. Light is pumped through the liquid, which excites the laser light to a certain wavelength.

Dyes have advantages over gas and solid-state lasers. Like solid-state lasers, the dye is easier to contain and control than a gas laser. Dyes can be pumped and changed while the laser is working, tuning the laser light to different wavelengths as needed. The molecules in the dye are also more complicated than the atoms found in gas and solid-state lasers. This allows dye lasers to produce a wider range of wavelengths than gas and solid-state lasers.

This is a high-energy laser that is used to shoot down rockets and artillery shells.

CUTTING EDGE

As long as a pump source puts energy into a laser, in theory, any source of energy can be used. If a lot of energy is created by the pump source, the energy of the laser will be very powerful. Scientists have suggested that a nuclear bomb could pump a laser beam strong enough to destroy missiles in space. The downside of such a powerful pump is that it could only be fired once and would be very dangerous.

A disadvantage of dye lasers is that the complicated organic molecules in the gain medium can break down under the energy from the laser's pump source. The liquid must be changed regularly to keep the gain medium fresh. Despite these problems, dye lasers can excite the light of the laser very quickly, producing a very powerful beam from very little energy compared to other lasers.

BIOLUMINESCENCE AND LASERS

Some living things can create their own light in a process called bioluminescence. Organic materials are already used as gain mediums in dye lasers. Scientists have made living lasers by injecting fluorescent dye beneath a layer of **cells** and shining a light pulse into that dye. The light excites the atoms of the dye, producing a tiny laser beam.

We have already seen that light is an electromagnetic force, just like infrared light, microwaves, and radio waves. These are all forms of invisible energy that have longer wavelengths and less energy than visible light. We can also make lasers that produce invisible light such as ultraviolet, x-ray, and gamma ray beams.

EXCIMER LASERS

An excimer laser is an ultraviolet laser. Skin or other organic materials easily absorb the ultraviolet light of excimer lasers. The laser vaporizes the top layer of skin, without damaging the layers beneath it. This makes excimer lasers excellent for medical procedures in which a top layer of skin must be burned off without harming the skin beneath it. This type of laser is used for delicate work such as laser eye surgeries.

XASERS

An x-ray laser, called a Xaser, provides an even higher energy beam than an excimer laser. X-rays can travel through soft tissues, such as skin and muscle, but not hard tissues like bone. This allows doctors to take pictures of skeletons, helping them check for broken bones.

GAMMA RAYS

Gamma rays have a much smaller wavelength than x-rays. Scientists could use them to probe at the smallest things in the universe, like atoms. Gamma rays might be used to push atoms so close together that they join, creating a burst of energy we call nuclear fusion. Gamma rays take a lot of energy to make and are dangerous because they deliver so much energy in such a small space they can kill living cells. For this reason, no gamma ray laser has been built.

Lasers large enough to join atoms need a lot of power and a large space in which to operate.

Lasers used in electronics and communications can be smaller than the head of a pin.

CHAPTER 3

WHAT LASERS CAN DO

Laser light is tuned to a particular wavelength, is contained in a tight beam, and carries a lot of energy. Scientists have turned lasers into a number of useful tools.

BURNING, MELTING, AND WELDING

Laser light delivers a lot of energy in a very small space. That energy, when absorbed, can produce enough heat to vaporize small sections of rock or melt metal. One of the first uses of lasers was to burn and melt things. Lasers could make more precise cuts than were possible with saws or presses. They could also weld, or stick, metal together.

DISTANCE AND SPEED

Light travels at 186,000 miles (299,300 km) per second, so measuring how long laser light takes to travel from one point to another allows the distance between the two points to be calculated. The best laser instruments can measure a distance of many miles to within fractions of an inch.

Lasers can also tell us how fast an object is moving. Laser light pointed at a moving object bounces off as waves. The speed at which the object is moving and the way in which it is moving determine the wavelengths of the laser light. By measuring the changes in the wavelengths of the light, it is possible to figure out the object's speed.

Industrial lasers are useful for cutting, etching, or welding metal.

MOVING LIGHT

Light from approaching objects has shorter wavelengths and a blue tone, while light from departing objects has longer wavelengths and a red tone. Astronomers have observed that the light of galaxies outside our own have a red tone. This means that these galaxies are speeding away from us. Therefore our universe is expanding, or getting ever bigger.

All substances absorb light in different ways. This is how people see colors. A red brick absorbs all the colors of white light, except for red, which it reflects. When a laser light is shone at an object, it is possible to figure out what the object is made of by studying the light that is reflected back. This process is called spectroscopy.

READING REFLECTIONS

Reflected laser light can also tell us how hot something is. Heat is energy, and the energy changes the laser light as it is reflected. This makes it possible to measure the temperature of distant things, such as clouds.

The ability to detect changes in reflected laser light is how lasers "read." Barcode readers work by shooting a laser beam across the black and white barcode stripes, while a detector in the reader notes changes in how that light is reflected. The barcode reader can detect differences between tiny markings and widths that most humans cannot see. This enables people to put a lot of information into a small area, such as a barcode, that a laser can easily read.

CUTTING EDGE

Barcodes were created in 1948, and the first barcodes used ink that glowed under ultraviolet light. A barcode reader could detect the glow and read the code. It then sent the code to a database that called up information about the barcode's product. The downside of ink barcodes was that ultraviolet ink is expensive and fades quickly. Barcodes detected by lasers became more popular because they could read barcodes printed in regular ink.

Lasers can read and transfer information faster than the human eye. Barcodes put this to work by allowing the laser to scan complicated information that a computer can read.

The more energy a laser uses, the more powerful it is. A laser pointer does not burn skin or reach to the moon, but a very powerful laser could. Laser power is measured in watts (W).

MEASURING LASER POWER

A watt is a unit of power that describes how much energy is produced or used in a set period of time. For example, a 220-pound (100 kg) person climbing up a 10-foot (3 m) ladder in 5 seconds uses about 600 W of energy. The energy lasers use can be measured in milliwatts (one-thousandth of a watt, shown as 1 mW), megawatts (1,000 watts, or 1 MW), or even higher, gigawatts (1,000,000 watts or 1 GW). These lasers are ranked by power from lowest to highest:

- Laser pointer: 1–5 mW
- DVD player: 5–10 mW
- High speed CD-ROM burner: 100 mW
- A laser able to burn through a CD case and the CD inside in 4 seconds: 400 mW
- A laser able to cut metal: 1–20 W (1,000 times more powerful than a laser pointer)
- Surgical laser: 30–100 W
- Industrial laser cutting: 100–3,000 W
- Laser able to join hydrogen atoms: 700 terawatts (700,000 GW)

The amount of energy used by a laser also depends on how long it is switched on for. A laser can produce enough power to burn a hole through metal. But, if the laser is turned on for just a fraction of a second, the total amount of energy needed to work a laser is actually quite low.

TO THE MOON

NASA's *Apollo 11, 14,* and *15* astronauts set out retroreflectors on the moon's surface. Retroreflectors are special mirrors that reflect beams of light directly back at the light source. Observatories on Earth can shine a 2.3–W laser at these retroreflectors and detect reflected light returning 2.5 seconds later (the time light takes to travel to the moon and back). Out of the 100,000,000,000,000,000 photons aimed at the reflectors, only one photon returns every few seconds.

CHAPTER 4

LASERS IN OUR LIVES

When lasers were first invented, scientists were unclear exactly how to use them. However, as scientists explored the things lasers could do, people found many ways to use them.

PHOTODETECTORS

Around the same time lasers were invented, Dr. John Shive (1913–1984) at Bell Labs invented photodetectors. These are devices that generate an electric current when hit with light. Photodetectors can "see" changes in light. They began to be used in conjunction with lasers, which provide a concentrated beam of light. When the light strikes a surface, such as a piece of paper, the photodetector reads what is on the paper by measuring the difference in the light reflected back to it.

The development of photodetectors and lasers meant that lasers could be used in devices to read data stored in a very small space. This led to the development of CDs and DVDs, which contain small pieces of information marked on the surface of the disks. CDs and DVDs store huge amounts of information in a very small space. More than 700 million pieces of data can be found on a CD, and nearly 10 billion bits of data can be found on a DVD. A CD or DVD player shines a laser on each piece of data and reads it by detecting the changes in the reflected light.

Laser tag started as a military training program in the late 1970s.

LASER TAG

As well as providing practical uses, lasers can be a lot of fun. By the 1980s, not only were people listening to music on CDs, they were playing laser tag. Laser tag weapons do not hurt anybody, but detectors in the weapons can tell when people have been hit by the beam of laser light. This allows people to battle each other harmlessly.

LASERS AT WORK

Lasers are good for business. Not only can lasers cut and weld things very precisely, laser readers allow businesses to keep track of goods by using barcodes. This means that stores can move products through cash registers quickly, and businesses can store their data easily on laser-read disks.

USES IN INDUSTRY

The ability of lasers to measure things with great precision also helps in many areas of business. Construction companies can more precisely measure what they are building. Mining companies can use spectroscopy to see how much precious metal is in their rocks. Printing companies can use lasers to engrave designs on printing plates and to burn words directly onto paper. Lasers can also scan objects, measuring them precisely. This has made it possible to make computer models, and then copy them using laser-guided machines.

SAFETY

Lasers are powerful tools, so people working with lasers must take care to make sure accidents do not happen and injuries do not occur, especially eye injuries. Signs warn workers to avoid areas where powerful lasers are used. People are trained to use lasers safely. They are told not to wear watches or jewelry that could accidentally reflect laser light. Special eye goggles, made of material that reflects the laser's particular wavelength of light, are worn to protect eyes.

Handheld laser pointers, while useful for pointing at diagrams or words on a board, can be dangerous because they are so easy to wave around. Government regulations ban the sale of laser pointers more powerful than 5 mW.

Lasers are being used more and more in industry for measurement and research. This scientist is carrying out research in a laboratory.

SECURITY

A laser pointed at a photodetector is an excellent way to detect when something obstructs the beam. This can send an alert if an object is in the way of something, like an elevator door. Hollywood likes to show laser tripwires in its movies, but in the real world, visible lasers are not used in this way. A person could easily reveal where the beams are by blowing smoke into the room. Security firms instead use infrared beams for their tripwires. These beams cannot be seen.

THREADS OF LIGHT

Fiber optic cables use refraction to guide lasers from one end of the tube to the other.

Of all the changes brought about by lasers, perhaps the biggest change has been sending a lot of information quickly over huge distances.

At the start of the twentieth century, people began to lay metal wires across continents and oceans. While this allowed people to send electrical signals faster than before, they were limited by what they could send. Worse still, the electrical signals broke down over long distances and could be interfered with or damaged by magnets or radio waves.

To send more information, people had to make bigger bundles of wires. Laser light travels as fast as regular light, but getting it from one place to another can be a challenge. Laser light moves in a straight line. It can be bent around corners using mirrors, but this can get complicated, and laser light loses energy if it reflects off too many surfaces. To help guide laser light around curves, optical fibers were invented.

FIBER OPTICS

Optical fibers are threads of glass. Once the light beam enters a glass thread, it bounces off the sides of the thread. Light travels all the way through the thread and comes out at the other end. These glass threads, called fiber optic cables, can guide light through a complicated path.

The information is coded as pulses of laser light before entering a fiber optic cable and being guided to the other end. Laser lights make their journey without breaking down. Once the laser reaches the other side, photodetectors turn the pulses of light back into the information that was sent. This allows information to be passed around the world. We can download music or talk to distant friends thanks to laser light.

CUTTING EDGE

A **semiconductor** laser has a semiconductor as its gain medium. These lasers produce an extremely small beam of laser light. This makes it possible to build a small device called a **diode**. Semiconductor lasers are excellent for reading and writing information at microscopic levels. They are also perfect for sending laser beams into fiber optic cables.

CHAPTER 5

CUTTING-EDGE USES

While we often think of lasers as weapons, the military found that they were not useful in this way. However, lasers do help the military target things and make them easier to shoot. A laser can shoot a dot of light on a target, which gives a sniper something to aim at. Lasers can also be used by guided missiles. A laser pointed at the target bounces back light, which a sensor on a bomb or a missile can see. The bomb or missile can then change its course toward that reflected laser light to precisely hit the target.

LIDAR

By aiming a laser at something and measuring the light that returns, lasers can also detect where objects are located, in which direction they are moving, and how quickly. This makes lasers an effective radar system. Radar bounces radio waves off objects to locate them. The laser version of radar is called lidar, which stands for "Light Detection and Ranging."

Lidar has smaller wavelengths and can detect finer details than standard radar. Lidar can identify aerosols, which could represent a biological weapon. Close range lidar has been used to map terrain. One day, lidar may enable military vehicles to drive themselves without a human at the wheel. Lasers would map the terrain as the vehicle drives, which would help it avoid obstacles.

This laser fired by the Starfield Optical Range in New Mexico helps measure the atoms in Earth's upper atmosphere.

MISSILES

To avoid being hit by a guided missile, the military makes potential targets less light-reflective. This can be done by painting them with a special kind of black paint. White objects reflect all colors, while black objects absorb all colors. When missiles hone in on reflected laser light, black objects reflect less light. This makes them more difficult to detect.

Many of the ways in which lasers are used by the military are also useful for ordinary people in their daily lives. Laser range-finders now measure rooms in houses and can project a line of light on a wall to help people mark where they should paint. The police use lidar to catch traffic offenders, and meteorologists (weather scientists) use it to analyze the moisture in the air, which helps them predict the weather.

LASERS IN MEDICINE

Breakthroughs provided by lasers have made surgery easier and more effective. Tiny lasers are fixed to the end of an endoscope. This is a long, thin camera that can be put inside a small cut or hole in the body and moved through the blood stream or other internal passages. Endoscopes have been used to find obstructions such as polyps in intestines or kidney stones. Once the doctor sees the obstruction on the camera, the laser can go to work, cutting the kidney stone so it can pass harmlessly out of the body. The heat of the laser also cauterizes (sears) any cuts and keeps them from bleeding.

CUTTING EDGE

If you think you may be sick, breathe on a laser! Scientists have developed a laser, called a laserlyzer, which can "smell" the molecules in a person's breath. Every different molecule absorbs light at a different frequency, allowing the laserlyzer to take a "molecular fingerprint" of a person's breath. By analyzing the molecules in the breath, it can detect a variety of infections, diabetes, and even cancer.

Lasers are being used on our streets, from the police officer seen here measuring the speed of passing cars to engineers taking measurements for road construction.

Lasers have been very useful in measuring the world around us. Lidar can help meteorologists measure weather patterns and make more accurate predictions. Lasers used in conjunction with satellites in space provide us with very accurate maps of our planet. Laser technology also helps people detect the first warnings of natural disasters.

AVALANCHE!

When dealing with the threat of avalanche, it is important to know how deep snow is on a mountain. The traditional method of using a yardstick to measure snow is not reliable, as snow

Lasers are used to measure volcanic ash in the atmosphere after eruptions.

CUTTING EDGE

Scientists have been looking at ways lasers could help make rain. In theory, laser pulses could excite nitrogen and oxygen atoms in the atmosphere, which would make them break up and form nitrogen oxide and ozone. This effect cools the atmosphere, allowing moisture to turn from a gas to a liquid in the air, forming rain. Currently, the effect is too small to be useful, but scientists are looking at ways to make it more powerful.

depth varies widely from place to place. It can also be dangerous, because people must walk around in the snow, measuring areas that could be hit by an avalanche. Today, scientists use a handheld laser device that shoots pulses of light at a mountain slope. By looking at how the light bounces off the snow and back to the receiver, this device can measure a 10-foot (3 m) deep snowpack to the accuracy of 0.5 inch (1.2 cm). It can send thousands of pulses over a wide area, making many different measurements.

VOLCANOES AND EARTHQUAKES

Scientists can use lasers to detect the ground moving, to the precision of a fraction of an inch, whether it is movement along a fault line or the bulging side of a volcano. These measurements can help scientists predict when the next earthquake might strike or the next volcano might erupt.

LASERS IN SPACE

Lasers are great for measuring distances precisely and identifying moisture in clouds or pollution in the air. Space is an excellent place to look down on Earth and observe its atmosphere, and lasers are especially useful for this.

CATS

NASA's Cloud-Aerosol Transport System (CATS) is a small instrument that was launched in January 2015 and installed on the International Space Station (ISS). CATS fires laser pulses at Earth and detects the photons that are reflected back from the planet. Meteorologists use CATS to measure tiny particles in the air at different levels of Earth's atmosphere. By doing so, they can analyze the makeup and movement of clouds.

COMMUNICATION

NASA is also looking at the use of lasers to communicate through space. In January 2013, NASA used a laser to beam an image of the *Mona Lisa* painting from Earth to the Lunar Reconnaissance Orbiter (LRO), 240,000 miles (390,000 km) away. Around the same time, a laser signal was sent 15 million miles (24 million km) from Earth to the planet Mercury, where the *Messenger* spacecraft picked it up. Lasers could soon act as backup communication for radios on satellites and spacecraft, keeping them in touch with Earth.

SPACE LASERS ON EARTH

An excimer laser made by NASA to measure Earth's ozone layer has been turned into a medical device that could be inserted into a person's bloodstream. The ultraviolet laser can safely burn away obstructions in arteries without harming healthy cells. This helps prevent heart attacks.

CUTTING EDGE

The ISS may become armed with a laser to shoot at threats in space, such as pieces of space junk like old satellites and abandoned rockets. In orbit, these objects travel at speeds of up to 22,370 miles (36,000 km) per hour, which would damage the space station. A 100,000–W ultraviolet laser could blast these objects. It would vaporize part of the object, and the force of the blast would push the rest of it out of harm's way.

On board the ISS, CATS fires laser beams into Earth's atmosphere to detect changes in it. It does this by measuring how the light changes when it is reflected back.

CHAPTER 6

BEYOND THE CUTTING EDGE

Lasers have been with us for fewer than 60 years, but already they have had a great impact on our lives. Technology changes over time. Devices become smaller, more powerful, and cheaper to build. We will all probably have many more laser devices in our lives in the future.

LASERS IN OUR HOMES?

Lasers can already beam bright videos on the sides of buildings. Advertisers use these projectors to make huge, eye-catching displays. This technology is now available in homes; instead of a flat-screen television set, a small laser projector can turn a living room wall into a home theater.

Just as barcode readers can read changes in laser light as it bounces off a surface, similar readers can allow people to interact with laser displays. The technology already exists to project the image of a computer keyboard onto a surface like a tabletop. As the user presses the image of the keys on the tabletop, the information is transmitted to the device that writes the words.

Lasers can also project light in three dimensions (3-D), creating holograms. Everything you see is light reflecting off objects. A system in which directed laser beams are bounced off the air, using something like smoke or dust, could be invented to produce an image that looks as solid as the real thing.

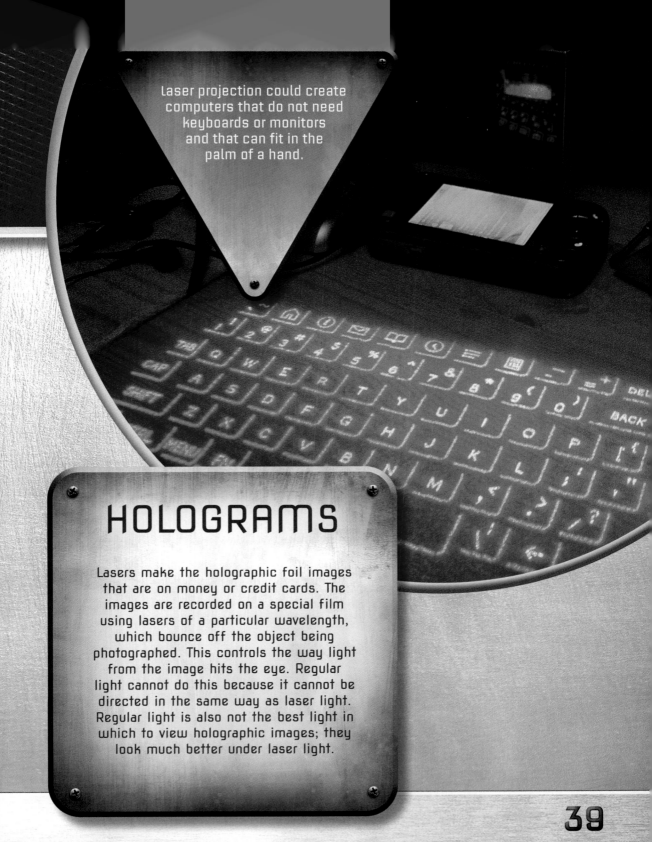

Laser projection could create computers that do not need keyboards or monitors and that can fit in the palm of a hand.

HOLOGRAMS

Lasers make the holographic foil images that are on money or credit cards. The images are recorded on a special film using lasers of a particular wavelength, which bounce off the object being photographed. This controls the way light from the image hits the eye. Regular light cannot do this because it cannot be directed in the same way as laser light. Regular light is also not the best light in which to view holographic images; they look much better under laser light.

People in industry, in science, and in the military will continue to research lasers and explore their potential. Much of the military's cutting-edge research is top secret, but we can expect them to push the limits of their lasers. Lasers will also become powerful enough to use as weapons in their own right.

WEAPONS, MEDICINE, AND INDUSTRY

In 2015, a German defense company unveiled a weapon that used lasers to shoot down enemy drones. The system uses four high-energy lasers mounted on a turret. The four lasers fire at once, producing one single, highly powerful beam.

Doctors hope to use miniature lasers to target cancer cells. They could be so tiny that microscopic machines called nanobots could carry them. The nanobots would travel through a person's bloodstream to the area affected by cancer. The lasers would target the cancerous cells.

In industry, laser scanners will produce computer models of objects more quickly and accurately, and laser cutters will make objects thinner and finer than ever before.

CUTTING EDGE

Thanks to lidar, Google has already built a car that can drive itself. Detectors in the car's roof help the computer driver keep the car in the correct lane, avoid obstacles, and not hit pedestrians or other cars. If we all had self-driving cars, we could work or sleep during our journeys, or call for a car and have one show up on our driveway. That would bring about big changes to our cities and the way we live.

This device uses two lasers to scan an object in order to make a 3-D model. By shooting at different angles, the two lasers combined produce very accurate measurements.

Scientists rely on lasers to help explore and explain the mysteries of the universe. Their research is pushing laser technology to new extremes. Lasers will be used in space exploration to help improve communications between Earth and space vehicles. They will also be used to accurately map space objects and analyze what they are made of.

In the Laser Interferometer Space Antenna (LISA) project, NASA and the European Space Agency (ESA) want LISA to look for gravitational waves, which have extremely long wavelengths. To do this, three spacecraft need to be spaced 3.1 million miles (5 million km) apart and yet still work together. Lasers will allow the three spacecraft to communicate.

The Paranal Observatory in Chile shoots a laser in the sky to create an "artificial star." Other observatories look at this star and monitor how Earth's atmosphere distorts their observations.

RECREATING THE SUN

Lasers are being used to create temperatures hotter than the core of the sun. Scientists at the National Ignition Facility hope to use lasers to smash hydrogen atoms together, fusing, or joining, them to form helium. This will copy the nuclear fusion that takes place in the center of the sun.

NEW MATTER

Lasers have also been used to cool substances to near absolute zero (–459.67 degrees Fahrenheit or –273.15°C). By tuning the wavelength of laser light to match the vibration of atoms, lasers can slow the atoms' vibrations until they are almost still. This removes almost all of their heat energy, making them colder than the vacuum of outer space. This process changes the atoms from a solid to a new form of matter called a Bose-Einstein condensate. This research is helping scientists better understand how the universe works and opens the possibility for bigger discoveries in our future.

BIG BANG

The most powerful laser in the world was fired at Osaka University in Japan in July 2015. This laser fired 2 petawatts (2,000 trillion watts, more than 1,000 times the world's electricity use) of energy to recreate the conditions of the **Big Bang**. It fired for only one-trillionth of a second, which is how it was able to generate such a burst of energy without using much power.

INTO THE FUTURE

Lasers depend on light, one of the building blocks of the universe. As people came to understand how the universe works, they were able to invent lasers. Lasers then gave people the tools to measure things more precisely, make objects less expensively, and communicate more quickly. Lasers helped further scientific research, which allowed people to understand the universe even more.

SCIENCE FICTION TO REALITY

A technology that had been science fiction fewer than 100 years ago now plays many important roles in our daily lives. It helps us listen to music, connect with distant friends and family, explore space, and push the extremes of hot and cold. It is amazing to see how far technology has come, but inspiring to imagine how much farther it could go.

It is difficult to predict what the future will bring in the next 60 years. As long as we have imagination and are motivated to explore, research, and experiment, we will continue to push cutting-edge technologies in unexpected ways, creating a remarkable future for us all.

CUTTING EDGE

Scientists at the Lawrence Livermore National Laboratory, in California, estimate that their 1 petawatt laser could shoot laser pulses into space. The beams could be detected by a civilization on a star up to 50 light-years away. In the years to come, scientists searching for extraterrestrial life may look for laser-light signals as signs that someone out there might be trying to say "hello!"

At listening stations aimed at the stars, messages from alien worlds might come to Earth as laser light rather than radio signals.

GLOSSARY

atoms the smallest particles of matter, from which molecules are made

Big Bang the moment at the start of the universe when all energy and matter in the universe exploded out of an extremely small and extremely hot point

cells the smallest functional parts of living things

chemical reaction the reaction of two substances to one another, changing their atoms or molecules

diode an electrical device that sends electricity or light in one direction

dopant an element added to a substance to alter its properties

electromagnetism a force created by the interactions of electric currents and magnetic fields

frequency the rate at which something repeats

gain medium part of the laser through which energy from the pump source is run. Atoms of the gain medium are excited by the energy, turning the energy into light of a particular wavelength

magnetism a force produced by the flow of electrical charge in objects

molecules particles made up of more than one atom

organic containing atoms that are often found in living things

semiconductor a substance that sometimes conducts electricity and sometimes does not, depending on certain conditions

solvent a liquid in which other substances dissolve

wavelengths distances between the crests of two waves

FOR MORE INFORMATION

BOOKS

Billings, Charlene W., and John Tabak. *Lasers: The Technology and Uses of Crafted Light* (Science and Technology in Focus). New York, NY: Facts on File, 2006.

Jacobson, Ryan, and Glen Mullaly. *How Lasers Work* (Discovering How Things Work). Mankato, MN: Child's World, 2011.

Wyckoff, Edwin Brit. *The Man Who Invented the Laser: The Genius of Theodore H. Maiman* (Genius Inventors and Their Great Ideas). Berkeley Heights, NJ: Enslow Elementary, 2014.

WEBSITES

Find out about the science of light and lasers, featuring articles and experiments at:
www.optics4kids.org/home

For informative articles, videos, experiments, and quizzes visit:
www.physics4kids.com/files/light_laser.html

Discover more about the science behind lasers at:
science.howstuffworks.com/laser1.htm

Learn how lasers are helping explore space at:
spaceplace.nasa.gov/laser

INDEX